To Hope and Fly

Leah Guzman Aldana

Presentation by *BookLeaf Publishing*

Web: www.bookleafpub.com

E-mail: info@bookleafpub.com

ISBN: 9789357612012

First edition 2022

DEDICATION

To Leonardo, Laramie, Jacob and Arielle.

PREFACE

A set of reflective poems inspired by nature, faith and childhood. The book is divided into four seasons and seeks to portray the sights and experiences of different times of the year, as well as emotions felt at different life stages.

Spring

The soft glow as the sun goes down
Marks the end of another day.
Do you welcome the approaching morn,
Or do you bid it stay away?

The blossom falls gently to the ground,
Settling like a blanket of snow.
Emerging leaves to the scene bring life,
Whilst children play and watch flowers grow.

Life is full of mountains to climb
But the summit's view takes your breath away.
Have you worries, anxieties, cares?
Cast them on Jesus at the dawn of each day.

A Mother's Love

Who can describe the love of a mother?
It comforts us unlike any other.
Tears are wiped and gone is fear
Whenever we sense our mother's near.

From the first cry her arms surround,
Her soothing voice a familiar sound.
The warmth of her body against the cold air,
Unconditional love which cannot compare.

A broken toy, a stumble or fall;
She consoles and calms us when we call.
God made our mother to love and care,
We know that she will always be there.

Lessons we learn when our mothers teach
Make us believe nothing's out of reach.
She encourages, is our help and guide,
Then watches as we grow, with pride.

When we have become fully grown
It's time for us to go out on our own.
We'll never forget the lessons she taught us
And all the years of joy she brought us.

Safe in the knowledge we're well prepared
To apply to our lives the wisdom she's shared.
We'll pass it on to the next generation,
Praying they spread joy and love to the nation.

The Fairy Child

Soft and delicate the fairy child
Stepped down from her treehouse out to play.
Her fine blonde hair, straggling wild
And beads of colour on it lay.

Through the trees the child did run,
Her shouts of happiness filled the sky.
The other infants shyly peeked out
And down from the branches did fly.

Hopping among the sweet-smelling flowers,
Gentle fragrance filled the air.
How beautiful the childhood innocence
Of those little fairies good and fair.

New Birth

Spring is a season of new birth
With buds breaking out upon the earth.
Lambs frolic in their soft curly fleece,
And hope in the air brings feelings of peace.

Daffodils blow in the gentle breeze,
Green is emerging on the trees,
Hibernating animals wake from their rests
And birds become busy building their nests.

At Easter we celebrate resurrection day;
How Jesus the punishment for our sins did pay.
He died on the cross for the sake of us all,
Giving new birth to all who on His name call.

New life and a chance to begin again
Is offered to children, women and men.
The new creation will start to show
As the Fruit of the Spirit continues to grow.

Sweet Dreams

Sweet baby girl upon your bed,
Tired from a day of learning and growing,
Rest now, safe as dreams fill your head.
The love in my heart is overflowing.

Summer

Waves crashing upon the sand,
Children playing hand in hand,
Shouts of glee, squeals of delight,
Fishermen watch as the gulls take flight.

Games and barbeques upon the beach,
People swimming out of reach,
Donkey rides and sculptures of sand,
The distant sound of a Mexican band.

Twilight draws nigh, this summer's day ends;
It's time to bid goodnight to friends.
The children snuggle down in bed,
Excitedly awaiting the day ahead.

Rocks

Little boy so full of adventure
Ready to go out and explore.
Run ahead with bucket in hand
As we head down to the shore.

The rocks are there all piled up high,
He reaches up to touch the sky
Then climbs on up – one, two step, three,
As confident as a boy can be.

Rock pools full of glittering treasure,
His beaming face so full of pleasure,
"Come on Mummy, come and see!
Come and share the excitement with me."

A crab, a fish, some slimy rocks;
He spots a ship there in the docks.
A pirate ship, oh can it be?
There, look! It's heading out to sea.

The sea seems to stretch on forever,
We always have such fun together.
My precious boy so brave and daring,
Yet so inquisitive and caring.

On to the next pool, up he goes,
Never thinking to take it slow,
The more he climbs, the steadier he gets,
Giggling each time his feet get wet.

The water's cold but never mind,
The boy just wonders what he'll find.
An anemone or hermit crab?
A day with him is never drab.

The day has gone, time to head back;
He clambers down the rocky stack.
His energy dwindles but his smile stays –
An emblem of the happiest of days.

Wildflower

A delicate beauty, it grows wild and free,
With paper-thin petals that call to the bee.
Bright colours so vibrant against darkened sky,
Bringing hope to all who are wandering by.

Sunflower Smiles

A crown of yellow
Like a lion's mane.
Hazel eyes shining bright
Wide open to your surroundings.

Your face towards the sun
Standing tall and strong
Making your presence known
And offering friendship to all who draw near.

Your innocence and joy
Are evident to see.
Your smile is contagious
Melting even the hardest heart.

The bees are at home
Among your bright petals.
You follow the sun as you grow,
Taking time to reorient and rest at night.

Moonlit Adventure

Into the woods she softly crept
Whilst the rest of her household soundly slept.
Where she was headed, she did not know
But onwards she did swiftly go.

Down the long passage between the trees,
Her nightgown fluttering in the breeze.
Such freedom one can rarely find,
An escape from the daily grind.

A tawny owl hooted in the tree,
The pathway she could barely see.
But treading deftly she carried on
As graceful as a floating swan.

She found herself in a moonlit glade,
At no point did she feel afraid.
She reclined upon a bed of moss
And drew the bracken leaves across.

Nocturnal animals shyly came,
No night would ever be the same.
She watched in quietude and delight
As fawns grazed and the bats took flight.

And by and by, at break of day,
She witnessed a majestic display,
A sunrise of yellow, purple and red
Painted up above her head.

Her heart alive, she felt such awe,
Humbled and thankful for what she saw.
She stood in silence then turned to go,
Basking in the sun's soft glow.

She tiptoed through her door of red
And softly climbed back into bed.
Safe she snuggled down to rest,
Dreaming of her night-time quest.

The Game

As you focus your mind on the game in play
Everything else seems to fade from view.
Your laugh of delight carries far across.
Each time you score, your heart leaps anew.

The wind as you run fills up your lungs.
Your cheeks are flushed in the glow of the sun.
The exhilaration as your feet take flight
Is further enhanced when your team has won.

The grass on your skin as you skid and slide
Makes you feel alive with the touch.
The bumps and grazes you wear home,
For the excitement are never too much.

Autumn

Giggle, shout, leaves about,
Throw them in the air.
Red, brown, yellow, orange carpet,
Branches become bare.

Crackle, crunch, what's for lunch?
Harvest fruit and nuts.
Walk along the muddy track
Treading in the ruts.

Chatter, shiver, all aquiver
Sat by firelight.
Marshmallows, toffee apples;
Whizz bang through the night.

Butterfly With Broken Wing

Butterfly with broken wing,
Why do you sit there so forlorn?
Whilst joyful birds begin to sing
Upon the first sign of dawn.

Such fond memories do you have
Of flying freely in the air,
But those moments have long since passed
And your beauty is masked by despair.

You cry disappointment for moments lost,
Your tears reveal your depth of feeling.
The future may seem void of hope
But consider, time and warmth bring healing.

Days full of sunlight will come again,
This pain will fade and hope will grow,
Your sorrow will turn into rejoicing,
And your weary countenance start to glow.

Do not despair when times are tough,
Keep your faith and cling to what is true.
Open your eyes to the beauty from above;
Once again you will rise into the blue.

Harvest Moon

Grand and resplendent the harvest moon,
Let's go to the cornfields hand in hand.
Come dance with me and bask in its glow
As we amble upon the farmer's land.

From the east it rises soon after sundown,
Radiantly orange from dusk till dawn.
Poised near the horizon, majestic it appears,
Let us rest by this haystack until the morn.

Full in the sky on this night mysterious,
Autumnal equinox days away.
A hint of this season's coming changes,
The moonlight shines as bright as day.

The moon illusion highlights its grandeur,
How large and close it seems to appear.
For now, I will savour this special moment,
Thankful for creation and your company here.

The Path

Have you ever wondered as you've wandered,
Cried and battled as you've pondered
In your mind, your thoughts convening,
On your search for truth and meaning?

Deepest thoughts you dare not share
But God can hear them, and He cares.
You're not alone, there is a way.
Will you trust in Him today?

Although it's not an easy ride,
The Holy Spirit will be your guide.
Will you trust God with your all
And go where He leads you with His call?

Hand over control, and freedom you'll find,
Light replacing darkness in your mind,
Knowing, no matter what comes your way,
Jesus is in your heart to stay.

Winter

At this time of year, it is easy to hide,
Snug in your duvet, all tucked up inside.
But venture outside and brave the chill air,
You may be surprised by what you see there.

Slow down, take long walks. Soon you will see
Just how exciting the winter can be.
The trees wave their arms, all covered in frost;
Showing no trace of the leaves they have lost.

The robins come searching for berries and seed;
Silently, we watch with delight as they feed.
Our stomachs are full, and what is the reason?
Mince pies and chestnuts, food of the season.

Cold winter evenings are oh so cosy,
Huddled by the fire with cheeks that are rosy.
At Christmas we focus on faith, peace and love,
Remembering the special gift sent from above.

Frost

Nights are colder, days are shorter,
Ice is seen upon the water,
Frosty evenings, twinkling stars,
Headlights shining from the cars.

Patterns on the window pane,
Icy breath and frozen rain,
Frosty plants, the mind perceives,
A sprinkling of sugar upon the leaves.

Papi

Those little faces look to you
To show them what is right to do.
They know with you it's lots of fun
And after work to you they run.

They jump on you and climb and tug,
You wrestle, throw them, catch and hug.
You teach them to plant bulbs and seeds
And you provide for all their needs.

You're always there, you have their trust
That you'll protect them if you must.
They know you're strong and oh so brave,
You take them exploring in a cave.

Thrilling bike rides and trips to the park,
You go for late walks in the dark
To see the big bright harvest moon,
You give them honey on a spoon.

In winter there's a snowball fight,
Hot chocolate's drunk by candlelight,
You pull them on a sledge of wood
And teach them what is right and good.

These are the memories that last forever,
The kind created in any weather,
From splashing in puddles and fun in the snow,
To the beach, barbeque and wherever we go.

They know they are loved by their dear Papi
And being with you, it makes them so happy.
So if ever you're down or someplace far,
Always remember how special you are.

A Simple Life

I sometimes dream of a simpler life;
Technology can be such a chore.
At times I wonder how it was
All that time before…

I imagine a time when speech was free
And the children played in the street,
When neighbours were all familiar
And would never fail to greet.

When gentlemen rose from their seats
As a lady walked into the room.
However, these days, the internet
Shows women as objects to consume.

What of the days when people ran free
And life was about love and sharing?
Is it possible to live like that now?
Will anyone be so daring?

Each person has a story to tell,
No matter the rank of the man.
The smallest decision may change life forever;
Beware of what your choices can.

The times when people travelled the world
With just the clothes on their back.
Incredible to feel so wild and free,
Yet often those feelings we lack.

I pity those who base their lives
On material goods they possess.
How easy it is to fall into that trap,
As I have at times, I confess.

For who can buy the love of another?
When money has dwindled and gone,
You will see the people who mean the most
And true friendship will go on.

Generations

When generations cease to mix
Imagine how much will be lost.
I fear that if we stay apart,
Society will bear the cost.

How quickly it seems some younger folk
Dismiss the ideas of the old
As though their voices are unworthy.
How can they be so bold?

Does life experience count for naught?
Opinions may differ from one's own,
But it's so important to learn from those
Who in different times have grown.

Don't underestimate history,
The lessons it has to impart.
All generations can learn together
And listening is where we start.

The elderly are inspired by youth;
Energy can be contagious.
How vital these interactions are;
To deny them is outrageous.

And what of the benefit to the young?
To have mentors bestowing advice.
The lack of role models is evident,
And it's children who pay the price.

Intergenerational interactions
Are needed to grow and learn.
From selfish individualism
I implore fellow citizens turn.

Visit your elderly grandparents,
Show your neighbours you care,
Speak to all ages in your Church –
There is so much wisdom to share.

The Storm

In my darkest days I know You are near
Although the tidal waves do rear.
I cry out to You, my special friend,
The only One on whom I depend.

Overwhelmed and tired, I hear the waves roar,
But of Your love I can always be sure.
Through heartbreak and trials, You understand;
I just need to reach out and take Your hand.

I may feel battered by all the waves
But You truly are the One who saves.
You died for me at Calvary,
And trusting in You, I am set free.